Conscious Development Guide
for
EFT Tapping Practitioners

Conscious Development Guide
for
EFT Tapping Practitioners

============

Energy Therapy Exercises to Improve
Your Practice and Your Life!

ANNE I. MERKEL, PH.D., CNHP

**THE ARIELA GROUP PUBLICATIONS -
MINERAL BLUFF - GEORGIA**

ISBN: 978-0-9961262-2-9

Join us at these locations to learn more about our Energy Therapy Programs!

Practitioner Info: www.AnneMerkel.com

Coaching Services : www.ArielaGroup.com

Alchemist Anne Blog: www.AlchemistAnne.com

My EFT Coach Blog: www.MyEFTCoach.com

EFT & Energy Therapy Mastermind Groups:

www.arielagroup.com/mastermind

Practitioner Training & Certification:

www.arielagroup.com/goingdeeper

"The quality of the results is only as good as the facilitator's energetic filter is clear!"

CONTENTS

This book presents some easy-to-use exercises for Conscious Development based on Energy Therapy combined with traditional planning and development approaches for life or business. Use this tool as a guide to moving forward in your life and your practice as you also learn exercises that you can personalize and share with your clients.

PREFACE & ACKNOWLEDGEMENTS

In my early life I was not introduced to anything considered "alternative". My conservative parents offered me what they thought was safe, "scientifically proven", and in my best interests. It wasn't until I left home to attend university that I started noticing the options available to me in all areas of my life.

Undergrad days were difficult. I did not know myself. I had difficulty keeping my body in balance. Diet was a huge confusion. Mood swings were my reality. A back injury bothered me in times of stress. I often felt like a victim, but of what, or whom?

In graduate school I was blessed when a friend took me for my first chiropractic adjustment. I had never heard of a chiropractor, but after one adjustment the shooting pain in my back disappeared and I could stand up again after days of suffering. Why had I not known earlier about this wonderful modality? Why hadn't I been able to ease the pain when I first fell off of my horse years before? I became a believer and searcher of alternatives. Years later another chiropractor told me that I would be able to let go of my back brace and enjoy an active life for the rest of my life, unlike the prognosis of an earlier orthopedic surgeon.

Fast forward many years. Now I practice Energy Psychology and am a Certified Natural Health Professional. I offer many energy therapy modalities to my clients. I've studied side-by-side with physicians and other Health and Wellness Practitioners for thirty years to learn techniques such as Neuro Emotional Technique (NET), Applied Kinesiology (AK), Emotional Freedom Techniques (EFT), Eden Energy Medicine, Healing Touch, Reiki, Allergy Antidotes, among others. Blend this with my previous experience as an adjunct professor in twenty colleges and universities plus my corporate work in training and development for hundreds of business clients, and the result is the ME of today.

I've enjoyed partnering with Chiropractors, Coaches, Therapists, Naturopaths, and other Health and Wellness Practitioners since 1986. I hope that this guide will provide you some helpful tools for your own conscious transformation. And, if you would enjoy working one-on-one with me or learning how you can incorporate energy psychology tools into your own practice, please check out my six-month program for practitioners[1] or twice-monthly practitioner Mastermind series.[2]

I wish to humbly thank all of my teachers, guides, mentors, supporters, and champions through the years and my varied careers, who have guided me to follow my heart and passions... to ultimately be here sharing with you now.

 2015

---

[1] For more information go to:
http://arielagroup.com/energy-therapy-certification
[2] Go to: http://arielagroup.com/mastermind

INTRODUCTION

I like to laughingly say that I've lived several lives in this body. In many ways this is true. And, with each life I've lived it seems that I've encountered a "dark night of the soul" in a physical, mental, emotional, psychological, or all-of-the-above way.

Extreme life change can lead to transformation, if one has the right support team and tools. Each time my life crashed I gathered support around me and kept learning. As I became more seasoned in the "art of life change", I realized the best tools and practitioners for me. And each time I re-created my own life I attracted others around me who also needed support, and thus, my energy therapy practice was born.

I was trained as a Practitioner of NET/ Neuro Emotional Technique with my ex-husband, a very good chiropractor, and later learned EFT/ Emotional Freedom Techniques so that I could work on myself. I became a Reiki Master and also worked through the certification levels of Healing Touch and Touch for Health/ Applied Kinesiology. Along the way I utilized the services of practitioners of most of the holistic modalities, and for several years I have integrated Energy Medicine into my Energy Psychology practice. In order to hold a license and better support my clients with nutritional counseling and homeopathy, I've undertaken studies to earn a second doctorate in Classical Naturopathy.

My practice specialty tends to be in autoimmune disorders, however, I've worked with clients presenting with cancer, job issues, PTSD, relationship problems, chronic physical or emotional pain, self-sabotage, skin lesions, re-occurring negative cycles or patterns, neurological spasms, plus more. I've been successfully supporting my clients since the late 1990's, and I enjoy sharing multiple techniques based on specific individual need.

In 1986-87 I trained my first class of chiropractors and I've worked with physicians, therapists, coaches, and other Health and Wellness Practitioners ever since.

Most intelligent, highly-educated individuals bore easily, so I custom tailor each treatment or training program for the person and practice in order to share new tools and concepts, and to integrate them into an on-going treatment protocol and practice.

I've seen practitioners blossom and their practices bloom after they incorporate energy therapy into their lives and practices. And, the patients love the positive results and life-changing tools that they take away from visits. So, everybody wins... and heals!

This book works hand-in-hand with my Certified Energy Therapy Practitioner Program[3]. As you use this text you may focus on your own life first as you work through the exercises here. And you will see that

_____

[3] Check out: http://www.myeftcoach.com/energy-therapy-practitioner-training-certification/

your professional life and practice automatically fit into some of the categories as outgrowths of your full life vision.

The progression of processes and focus on clarifying the Vision, then creating a Plan with Priorities, and finally bringing it forth through Journaling seems simple, and yet it is profoundly life-changing.

The exercises found in this book are natural and allow for, no - require that you show up as your authentic SELF. You may have come across similar exercises and techniques in the past, however this is NOW and the way these tools are organized will gently bring forth from your innermost SELF the true Vision, Purpose, Plan, and Steps to move you and your practice past blocks or inner resistance that have held you back in the past.

I wish you the best as you journey the path of Conscious Life and Business Transformation, and as you continue to support the wholistic health and wellness of others.

For more information feel free to contact the author directly or refer to her website or blogs.

What others are saying about my support services:

"I enjoyed gaining an insightful reminder into what my passions about my work are. I also enjoyed identifying the characteristics and strategies that keep us excited about the goals we put in front of ourselves, and how to turn those goals into action."
-J.L./ V.P. Construction Corp./ Lexington, SC

"Anne, thank you again so much for your support, understanding, encouragement and guidance. You helped me rediscover my drive and what truly motivates me. You reminded me how important the way we feel and think is. Through the techniques you used during our coaching sessions you enabled me to control my thoughts and redirect my energies in a positive way. Because of this I was better equipped to navigate through a time of transition and I have achieved my major goals by applying your advice. I always felt your thorough dedication and the love you put into your work. I'm grateful for your warmth and genuine guidance."

-G.H./ Business Coach, Management Consultant/ Munich, Germany

"I LOVE your group coaching classes and will diligently put your advice to use! I have loved your work and feel you are an AWESOME teacher and mentor. You are an inspiration to me! I wanted to thank you for sharing all your gifts and putting yourself out there and achieving your goals you set for yourself. I KNOW and can FEEL you make a difference in thousands of people's lives every day, as one person touches another and another. Also when we heal ourselves, everyone is blessed by the experience. Again thank you for your support. Much love and great appreciation for all your classes. They have meant a great deal to me! MORE than you know!"

-M.J./ Wellness Consultant-Coach/ Mt. St. Helens, WA

TAKING YOUR DREAMS TO REALITY

Our society speaks of dreams, of manifesting our dreams, and bringing our dreams into reality. Our vernacular includes *wishing* and *wanting* and *setting intentions* of our desires.

If you use affirmations or even state your desires in the terms of "*dreams*", then what you might attract to yourself are more and more DREAMS. And if you constantly state "I *want*...", then you will continue to WANT.

So, let us start this section with semantics that state that you **CHOOSE** certain things, conditions, feelings, characteristics to be in your life... now and in the future.

I am convinced more and more each day that the REALITY that you create is based on setting energy in motion by clearly thinking, feeling, and then acting.

The way it used to work...

The "old paradigm" way of manifesting was by pushing and pulling our way to a set goal or destination. This "yang" process was the following:

BE CLEAR ➜ DO the WORK ➜ HAVE the RESULTS

Yes, we succeeded, often, to reach our goals. Sometimes we found the struggle energizing when the results were rewarding. Often the pain and sacrifice leading up to a perceived "success" left a burned out shell of the warrior who first started the journey.

Times have changed. Paradigms have shifted. New approaches and attitudes are required now.

The old model included a person playing a specific role.

BEing in a position to create a thought, nurture a dream, set a goal, the person started out by holding the form for the energetic of a clear goal.

Then came the traditional social pressure to **DO**, to take specific actions leading to the goal. If someone didn't appear to be busy enough, then something was wrong and that person was perceived as being lazy or not worthy of the final reward.

Finally, after the work was done and the outer tasks were performed, the person could **HAVE** the pleasure of experiencing the goal completed and its rewards. Sometimes that person was unable to enjoy or celebrate because of the amount of struggle it took to get to the goal.

This is how the **OLD** way of getting what we wanted in our society used to work for us. There are many reasons why this "force of will" or "Just Do It" approach doesn't work anymore for many individuals and segments of the population.

The BEST way now to create REALITY from your dreams...

Many of us have discovered a path to inner discovery and transformation. For me and for many of those who I coach and facilitate, it is impossible for us to go back to the way we once set and achieved goals.

Is this also true for you?

Are the old ways not working as they once did?

Creating from your dreams requires a new set of tools and a new way of looking at and **FEELING** the process.

The new process flow is confusing to some at first, and yet, it is the basis on which life as you know it was set from the beginning of time. The new flow goes along with the Universal Law of Attraction with the laws of Deliberate Creation and the Law of Allowing.

The Universal Law-based process is summed up in the following process flow:

BE CLEAR → FEEL RESULTS → DO Inspired Acts → HAVE Goal Results

In this approach, again it starts with someone **BEing** himself/herself and harboring a thought or dream. The normal flow of universal energy automatically starts the attraction process based on this thought.

In order to speed up the process one can then consciously go to the **FEELings of HAVEing** the desired end results already. The energetics start to swirl faster as the FEELINGS of attaining the end results are the focus. So, if you pretend that you already **HAVE the REALITY** that you want, then the

Universe seems to work even faster to bring this to you.

Instead of running around beating bushes all day or busily performing traditional tasks, the last phase here is an anticipatory waiting for the **INSPIRATION** of what **RIGHT tasks** should be performed to bring about the best results. You are guided as to what you must DO using this model.

(In traditional jargon I point out the "80-20 Rule", where typically 80% of the results come from performing just 20% of the actions.) In this Universal Flow model, you don't need to waste your time on the 80% of actions that bring no results. You can easily learn how to FEEL whether you are aligned with an action or not, and perform the tasks that feel good to you. Those that come up because you "have always done it that way" or because society tells you that you must do something in a certain manner, are dropped if they feel "wrong". Yes, it IS a process that must be learned, and is what I guide my clients to learn and practice so that it becomes second nature and is easy for them to discern whether to do something or not.

In the meantime, by following the **BE ➔ FEEL As Though You HAVE ➔ DO** model you can learn to wait for and feel the urge to act, and follow the inspired actions rather than forcing yourself to be a traditional workaholic. You can get the same results by exerting more inner FEELING energy and less outer strain and forced activity.

Also, to "amp up" the results, the best lubricant in the process of manifestation is that of GRATITUDE. When you are focusing on what you HAVE, then you can more easily attract more of that to yourself. Conversely, when you focus on what you DO NOT HAVE, then you attract THAT to yourself too.

Which do you prefer??

The subconscious mind doesn't discern the past – present – future; it reacts to feelings and gets used to feeling a certain way. You have the power to be living your dream or suffering in your own personal hell. So, as you **BE ➔ HAVE ➔ DO** remember to feel the emotions associated with gratitude as you bathe in the beauty of feeling that which you are creating. CHOOSE life with all of its FEELINGS. Speak and write about the gratitude - of what you have in the NOW REALITY, and also speak and write of your gratitude for the feelings you encounter in going to that NEW REALITY place and FEELING your NEW LIFE of abundance.

Later in the journaling section of this book there are guides to use that will automatically remind you of the importance of daily gratitude for what you have NOW. The journal exercises will help you to create an attitude of gratitude.

If you already know a meridian tapping technique, then apply that while feeling the desired results of your goal. This will amp up the vibration. And, since GRATITUDE is the key to success that not only reinforces the attraction of what you feel grateful for, but also automatically raises your personal vibration from one of a low frequency focus on lack to a high frequency appreciation of good things going on, then tap that into your subconscious!

Enjoy the process of attracting. Journal your thoughts, feelings, challenges, and results so that you can map your progress. This is a potent foundation to place into your daily NEW LIFE as you are creating it!!

KNOW YOURSELF FIRST

In this chapter you'll find an exercise that will help you to determine the focus of your subconscious mind so you will better understand what you are energetically attracting. It will explain how you consciously and subconsciously attract both what you desire and also what you would like to avoid. [4]

In subsequent chapters you will also be guided to use energy therapy tools to clear old detrimental patterns that no longer serve your best interests and desires.

---

[4] For a more detailed explanation of this Values Exercise including 2 hours of audio mp3 plus e-guide go to:
http://www.arielagroup.com/products/free_products.php

E-Valuating Yourself from the Inside -- Out

In my opinion, whenever you start a new program or a new year or a new stage of your life, it's important to know certain things before you waste your time setting goals or jumping into the new program or the new stage.

The things that you need to be clear about are:

- Who you are, and that relates to your values, beliefs, old habits, old patterns,
- What you want, because you can't attract anything unless you're clear about this,
- What you must do to get what you choose.

There are two steps to this.

1. The inner step is to identify your internal values and align your energies so that you're not in internal conflict.

2. The outer step is the one we're most familiar with, which is setting the goals or action steps.

In this section you will identify your internal values of what you desire as well as what you wish to avoid.

Evaluating What You Choose to ATTRACT into your life:

On a sheet of paper jot down ten emotions or values that you would like to have in your life to answer the following questions:

- What is most important to me in life?
- What do I really choose to feel in my life?

Consider this for awhile and jot down a list of everything that comes to mind. Next look for your top ten and focus on them for the rest of the exercise.

Prioritizing your values into the order of importance

Take the list of your ten emotions/ characteristics/ values and focusing on the first and second on your list, ask the following question:

"Which feels more important to me: Number 1 or Number 2?"

After you have made this decision, then take your new Number 1 and compare it to Number 3 asking:

"Which feels more important to me: The updated Number 1 or Number 3?"

Take the highest item here (which becomes Number 1) and then compare it to Number 4 saying:

"Which feels more important to me: The updated Number 1 or Number 4?"

Next set aside your Number 1 and follow this same process to identify your official Number 2.

After you have identified the exact priority of all ten of your values, then you will know, consciously, how you make your decisions and on what you base your decisions.

Re-write your Values list in priority order, and begin to look it over for any patterns, overlaps, contradictions, or other curious points that seem to jump out at you.

What happens when your values are set up for the wrong reasons?

In this first section you were guided to identify the values, characteristics, situations, or feelings that you choose to attract into your life. Then you prioritized them.

There are times when you may have set values or intentions of how you wish to feel based on past experiences that didn't feel good. You may have created a positive value, but it's based on negative experiences.

In order to get beyond that, you may need to do some energy work to clear out the old remnants and the old subconscious memory of the negative that caused you to choose these particular positive values in your life.

(If you are new to energy therapy, then be patient because I will guide you through a process at the end of the next section. And, if you wish to jump ahead, you may learn more about Classic EFT/ Emotional Freedom Techniques and using it on your own.[5])

_____

[5] For both audio mp3 and video support go to:
http://www.arielagroup.com/products/free_products.php

Identifying the Values or Conditions You Wish to Avoid

Now that you have identified the positive values you wish in your life, it is a good next exercise to identify values or feelings you wish to AVOID at all risk because these can cause subconscious self-sabotage and worse.

To start identifying the values, conditions, beliefs you wish to avoid, ask yourself the following questions:

- What is most important to avoid feeling in my life?
- What feelings do I really choose to avoid?
- What patterns may be occurring in my life around these issues I choose to avoid?

Make a list of your own "Negative Values" or Emotional Conditions or Issues that you Choose to Avoid. Let you mind wander and list everything in your reality that you choose to stay away from in your life or practice.

Prioritizing Your Negative Emotional Factors

Like you did with your positive values, now you will rank these aspects you choose to avoid by their significance or charge in your mind. Use the same exercise as the one you used for ranking your positive values.

To place them in order use one of the following statements:

- "I would rather avoid feeling __X__ than __Y__." (Compare the 1st & next on your list.)

- "I work hardest to avoid feeling __X__ over feeling __Y__."

Remember to take the highest or 1st on your list and compare it to each other item on your list. Then take the second highest on your list and compare it to each other item on your list, and so on until you have every negative value ranked by importance.

Clearing the Charge that Attracts

The next step is to clear out the charge you may have on each and every one of these negative emotional factors or values.

Start with your top negative value and use the simple meridian tapping technique that you will find on the next few pages to clear out the charge as you imagine the cases where this feeling lurks in your thoughts. Then go down the list. Some of the negative values will disappear as you dis-charge the top ones.

Please personalize the tapping sequence on the next page so that you may gain the most from it.

And to learn more, go to the free download audios and video[6] which will introduce the concept of meridian tapping and will show you the specific tapping points, the protocol, and what to say.

---

[6] For support go to:
http://www.arielagroup.com/products/free_products.php

N-hanced EFT Tapping Sequence for Clearing Charge Around Negative Values

Follow these sequences putting in appropriate words for your situation and tapping at the point indicated. For more information about WHERE to tap, please view the short video.[7]

And, throughout the sequence, remember to FEEL the issue you choose to avoid, and FEEL the emotion associated with this choice to avoid the issue at all cost. Feelings are of upmost importance in the process!

Karate Chop point:

Even though I have a fear about attracting this in my life . . .
I deeply and completely understand why I have this resistance.
On some level, I know why I am avoiding this feeling.

---

[7] Go to: http://www.myeftcoach.com/alternative-medicine/

I know that my subconscious is protecting me from being hurt.

Even though I really choose to avoid this in my life . . . and in the past this has felt really horrible to me . . . and the experience I had before was very uncomfortable to me . . . I really never choose to feel this again.

I choose to be free from this feeling or this situation.

I choose just the opposite of this old feeling or condition.

I choose to live a wonderful life, completely free of this old condition, this old thing that I am avoiding.

I can let go of the memory of this.

I can let go of the fear of attracting this into my life.

I can let go of even thinking about the possibility of attracting this into my life.

I choose to be safe from this condition and this feeling.

I know that I protect myself as best I can.

I know that I can let go of the charge around feeling this way.

I know I can let go of the charge around attracting this into my life.

I know I can let go of all charge so I absolutely am not magnetizing this to myself.

I am letting it go now.

I am clearing it out of my system now

I am moving on and letting it go, from my past, this old fear.

I'm giving myself the freedom to move forward without this.

Eyebrow point:

It makes me angry to think that I'm carrying this in my subconscious.

This is something that I really choose to avoid.

I feel it's time now to completely clear it and let it go.

Worry only keeps it in my subconscious.

I can completely let it go now.

I can feel peacefulness and have it totally gone.

Outer Eye point:

I am letting go of resentment about having this
charge in my system.
I resent that I had a bad experience in the past about
this.
I resent that I feel what I felt from bad past
experiences.
I resent that I put too much energy already into
avoiding this.
I resent that I have been held captive by this emotion,
this fear, trying to avoid this.
I can let myself freely let it go now.
It no longer serves me to carry this around.
Thinking about it or worrying about it only gives it
power.
The past is the past and I can let it go.
I'm ready to create a whole new scenario without this
old issue or this old feeling.
I'm letting it go now.

Under the Eye point:

I am claiming my personal power back now.

Trying to avoid this issue has just sucked my energy.

It hit me in the stomach, in the solar plexus.

It sapped my power and my energy.

It's caused me stress.

I choose to have peace of mind.

I choose to have clarity.

I choose to let this old feeling, the fear of this feeling,

go right now.

I'm letting it go.

Under the Nose point:

I really love myself.

I really respect myself.

I love my new visions for myself, my dreams and

intentions for myself.

I feel so potent sometimes . . . and it's time now to let

go totally of this thing I was trying to avoid.

It's absolutely time to let it out of my energy system

completely now.

I can totally forget about it, let it go completely now.

I can be free to flow freely without being held back by any old things I'm trying to avoid.

Chin point:

There have been times when I've been ashamed and embarrassed that I was so worried about this showing up in my life.
I've been embarrassed and ashamed when that old situation happened in my life that might have caused me to want to avoid it ever happening again.
I can let go of that.
I can hold my head up very proudly now.
I can go forward without fear.
I'm ready to go forward freely without anymore self-sabotaging.
It is time for me to feel good about moving forward in my life.
I'm letting go of any old beliefs that are holding me back.

Collarbone point:

I have felt fear about this condition coming into my life for too long.

I have been afraid.

I have been avoiding this feeling in my life.

I have been afraid and I've been avoiding attracting this situation into my life.

It's time to let go of the fear.

I don't need the fear anymore.

Feeling afraid does not serve me; it only holds me back.

I'm letting go of all fear around this situation.

I can let it go for good now.

I can take off the charge and it won't be in my system anymore.

I'm ready, willing and able to let it go.

It's time to clear it out.

Under the Arm point:

I have everything I need to be totally successful in my life.

I have everything I need to be happy and healthy and live a life of abundance.
I have everything I need to attract all the values I really want to have into my life.
Now is the time to let go of this issue that no longer serves me.
I'm ready, willing and able to let it go now.

Top of Head point:

I'm grateful that I have these wonderful tools to use now.
I am grateful that my wonderful subconscious has protected me up to this point.
I am grateful that I have cleared the charge on this issue and I know how to continue clearing any little residue that's left.
And so it is.

Other Values Issues to Consider

As you work with your own values and guide your clients and patients to go deeper, you must pay close attention to the many ways in which values can conflict and cause inner incongruencies and blockages that will result in self-sabotage, emotional and physical pain.

Positive Value ← // → Positive Value

Positive Value ← // → Negative Value

It is important to become congruent with each of these:

- Positive Values & their Priorities with each other and with your life
- Negative Values & their Priorities + Impacts on your life
- Positive Value versus Positive Value (conflicts)
- Positive Value versus Negative Value (conflicts)
- Negative Foundation under a Positive Value

Here are a number of related examples:

- **Positive Values & their Priorities:**

<u>Example:</u> Feeling that "being spiritual"(rather than "supporting my family well") needs to be #1 priority based on an old belief that spiritual people don't focus on making money. Tap away charge on this issue so that no "should's" govern your values, and you may notice your values shift priorities... or not.

- **Negative Values & their Priorities:**

Example: "Never wanting to be fat like X." – and yet, hating diet & exercise. Underlying energy under the "never wanting to be..." attracts just that. Tap away charge around both.

- **Positive Values in Conflict:**

Example: "Wanting to treat X number of clients." At the same time you "Only want to work 3 days per week." Maybe this doesn't seem possible in your belief system. Tap away all doubt so you are not held back.

- **Positive & Negative Values in Conflict:**

Example: Wanting to "Live like a rich person" versus "Hating certain greedy rich people" can cause you inner conflict. Tapping on all attitudes around rich people will help.

- **Negative Cause for Positive Value**

Example: Memories of being poor haunt you still so you set a value of attracting a lifestyle of plenty. Tapping is required here to dissolve the negative charge that is behind your positive value.

Example: Guilt about a bad relationship mistake leads to the creation of a value to attract the "perfect" relationship. Without tapping out the guilt and other issues around the failed relationship no new relationship will ever be near to "perfect". Tap through all aspects of the bad relationship that come to mind.

PERSONAL VISIONING

In the manifestation process you play with many thoughts and visions of what might be. In the process of active dreaming you can easily shift from one focus to another. As you do this you are mentally "trying on" the various thoughts, ideas, scenarios to determine which ones "fit" and which ones can be released.

In the process of visioning you play with swirling energies and often your intentions are not clear enough to truly manifest. You may have not yet defined the specifics of and have not grounded your dream. In order to send out the clearest message to the Universe or your subconscious mind of what you REALLY want to receive, you must be very clear in everything you ask for. "Ask and ye shall receive," has potent energy and in order to get what you REALLY want and what is best for you, it is best to be clear about and careful of what you request and around what you focus your intention and feelings.

Pure Potentiality

In the visioning process I endorse a focus on your innate sense of Pure Potentiality. This is not a focus on potential, per se, but is a focus on a vibrational frequency of Universal Flow and Universal Abundance.

- It is the state from which you manifest.
- It is the state from which all good things come.
- It's a total state of unlimited opportunity, abundance and infinity.
- It is the Universe.
- It's all that your human mind can comprehend as being total everything.
- It is God, some people would say.

In approaching your vision with this childlike sense of awe and wonder, and belief that everything is possible, then you can experience your vision growing and becoming tangible before your eyes.

Clarifying Your Vision

If you feel stuck and the idea of coming up with a clear vision seems like an impossible feat to you, don't panic or give up. Many people feel this way and find themselves in that same state of confusion, frustration, impatience, and then self-doubt.

To aid you on your journey there are some exercises explained and facilitated on a recording of a live TAPshop group energy therapy tapping call that is available to you.[8]

Creating Your Vision

One way to help you clarify your personal vision is to divide your life into various categories and then identify details related to each. Spending some time doing the following exercise will help you clarify your intentions for creating the NEW REALITY from your

----

[8] Go to: http://is.gd/GettingClear

Dreams. Focus primarily on yourself and secondarily on your practice.

I suggest that you go through the entire exercise with your personal life in mind first. Then go on to the next section, and with a clear mind go back through this exercise focusing on your practice and logging in the various points for your practice. You might then compare certain aspects of your life and practice that overlap or show similar patterns.

CREATE YOUR BEST SELF

1- List below, under each category, the three things/characteristics/group of issues that you absolutely CHOOSE and EXPECT in that aspect of your life,... things that you REQUIRE 100% to fulfill your dream. (You may list more than 3, but make sure you have at least this many.)

NEXT:

2- List three things/ habits/ feelings/ conditions that you absolutely DO NOT CHOOSE or that you would like to RELEASE from that aspect of your life, and that you will 100% REJECT from your NEW LIFE as you are designing it. (You will be guided to use a specific tool to help you let go of whatever you place into this category, so do not limit yourself.)

NEXT:

3- Now list "extra credit" details that would enhance your experience within that aspect of your life. These are Requests rather than Must Have's.

Spiritual Life:

MUST HAVE:

1-

2-

3-

MUST RELEASE:

1-

2-

3-

Extras:

1-

2-

3-

Personal Health:

     MUST HAVE:

1-

2-

3-

     MUST RELEASE:

1-

2-

3-

     Extras:

1-

2-

3-

Education:

MUST HAVE:

1-

2-

3-

MUST RELEASE:

1-

2-

3-

Extras:

1-

2-

3-

Recreation:

MUST HAVE:

1-

2-

3-

MUST RELEASE:

1-

2-

3-

Extras:

1-

2-

3-

Financial Status:

MUST HAVE:

1-

2-

3-

MUST RELEASE:

1-

2-

3-

Extras:

1-

2-

3-

Career, Job, Mission:

MUST HAVE:

1-

2-

3-

MUST RELEASE:

1-

2-

3-

Extras:

1-

2-

3-

Family:

       MUST HAVE:

1-

2-

3-

       MUST RELEASE:

1-

2-

3-

       Extras:

1-

2-

3-

Home:

MUST HAVE:

1-

2-

3-

MUST RELEASE:

1-

2-

3-

Extras:

1-

2-

3-

Ethics, Morals, Values:

MUST HAVE:

1-

2-

3-

MUST RELEASE:

1-

2-

3-

Extras:

1-

2-

3-

Now that you have a clearer idea of your desires for your NEW life in all major areas, with all of the NEW requirements and parameters, it is time to put that intention out so that the results can start to appear.

By reading your criteria regularly you are reminding your subconscious and sending out the "vibes" of attraction so that the abundance you most desire can flow to you and create this NEW LIFE from the inside out.

This vision of the NEW LIFE you are creating can also "keep you on track" so that you can discard or not fall back into old unbeneficial patterns.

We are often tempted to "back slide" into past habits. You might be comfortable with something that in reality is unhealthy for you, and still there is that old temptation to just fall back into the pattern again. By regularly reviewing your vision criteria you can keep yourself accountable to the NEW LIFE you are consciously creating. The exercise can be used as a tool to keep you on track and help you to Flow Forward.

And, in addition to checking back over your lists, there is much power in creating an artistic rendition of your vision for your future via a "Vision Board" or picture depiction of what your life will look like and feel like as it develops. This is a powerful process and need not include any words or text to bring forth results. Simply by pasting photos from magazines with which you resonate, you can create some powerful attraction energies. And, a gentle reminder... be clear about what you place into a Vision Board, because it will come to you![9]

_____

[9] For more info about my own Creativity Playshops go to: http://arielagroup.com/creative_playshops/playshops.php

Clarifying for Your Business = Energy Therapy Practice

Now that you have focused on your personal life, here is a separate section to list some specifics around your business life. Follow the earlier directions to jot down your details for the energy therapy business you are creating or the new look of your previous business as you integrate energy therapy into it.

My Practice:

MUST HAVE:

1-

2-

3-

4-

5-

6-

7-

8-

9-

MUST RELEASE:

1-

2-

3-

4-

5-

6-

7-

8-

9-

Extras:

1-

2-

3-

4- ·

5-

Personal Notes about My Practice:

MULTI-SENSORY VISION

Now that you've analyzed the aspects of your life using the left, analytical side of your brain, you can call in the creative right mind to use your senses to draw and enact your vision... in living color, sound, taste, smell, and touch![10]

First, think of yourself living in your "NEW life"...

Write a description of this NEW life – the spiritual aspects, your physical health, your education, your favorite forms of recreation, your financial status, your career/job/work, your family, your home, your ethics and attitudes about your life.

Describe the details, how you FEEL about each aspect; describe your sensory perceptions as you are LIVING this life you love.

---

[10] Access an audio mp3 that walks you through this exercise by going to: http://is.gd/MultiSensoryVision

Cover all of the senses so that you feel the temperature, smell the surroundings, touch and feel the reality of the walls of your home, feel the caring embraces of loved ones, enjoy the excitement or peace of mind having a fun-filled job or mission to perform, etc.

Take several shorter writing sessions if you need to, and write paragraphs about each of the life categories. (Remember that you can come back and shift some things around as your NEW Life vision continues to clarify for you.)

Focus on how you will _feel_ in each aspect of this "New Life" that you are creating. Write down all of the details as they come to you, and come back later to enter more aspects of this sensory vision.

With your intentions firmly set, communicated, felt, and regularly reviewed, these exercises for manifesting your NEW Life will start to show results in the shortest time possible. Enjoy the process!!

PLANNING FOR SUCCESS

Old paradigm planning used to place the outer actions before the inner actions. In this section we will guide you to shift your approaches from traditional to new paradigm planning with several inner and outer exercises.

It is still of value to make plans... when you are guided to do so.

I'll never forget how when I first put my wonderful home on the market and had a contract with 30 days until closing, I felt pressure to create the plan for what would happen next.

My intuition told me all was in the Divine Plan and that certain practical things might be handled while other tasks could be set aside.

I felt fine about setting up all of the closing details so that I was ready for the scheduled movers. I also felt fine about loading my pets into my newly manifested vehicle and heading west before the moving van, still giving myself several days to find the best place to live in my chosen new city.

My more traditional parents were very afraid for my plan. They insisted that there was urgency in finding a place to move. This was perceived by them to be much more serious of a matter than how I looked at it. (I knew how quickly in the past I had been able to manifest just the "right" place to live.) They had no faith, so they even bought the airline ticket to send me out to find and rent my next home. I flew out, found the perfect house for myself and my little family on the second day, and then flew back to close the house sale.

Well, the Universe, and I, on a subconscious level, had other plans in mind. It turned out that the house closing was postponed then, and then again, until finally I had to let go of my rental contract after paying thousands of dollars to hold a wonderful home where I never lived. If I had listened to my own intuition I would have saved money and energy. Hindsight is so wonderful!! I was driven into action by the fears of my parents. Next time I will listen to my own inner voice.

Often we are driven to make decisions and to take actions based on:

- Perceived Seriousness (by oneself or another)
- Fear (our own or that of another)
- Perceived or Projected Condition of Urgency
- Habit or Learned Protocol
- Perceived Growth of a Personal Threat to Ourselves

Usually when we are pushed to make a snap decision or quick purchase or immediate action it is best then to take the following steps:

Pause and Breathe.

Identify feelings within your body related to what you are being asked to do.

Ask yourself the following questions about your feelings regarding the action being presented – focus on the condition of you being asked, pressured, forced, enticed to perform the requested action:

- Does it feel light or heavy?

- Does it feel soft or hard?

- Does it feel fast-moving or slow/non-moving/paralyzed?

- Does it feel smooth or rough?

- Does it feel easy or hard?

- Does it feel cottony or sticky?

- Does it feel cool or hot or neutral?

- Do you feel open or contracted?

- Is your breathing even and normal or uneven and light/surface?

- Is your heart beating at a normal speed or is it beating quickly?

Do you feel comfortable or uncomfortable as you are being asked to take the action or make the decision?

Are you being pushed by FEAR around SERIOUSNESS, URGENCY, GROWTH of the issue or condition? Is this YOUR FEAR???

After following this exercise of feelings you can usually judge whether you are just being pressured into action or decision by another person and their fears, by savvy marketing people who want to push you into a purchase of something you may or may not need, or your own FEARS.

The bottom line on deciding when to make a decision or to take action is:

IF IT FEELS GOOD, DO IT!!*

(*based on the bulleted criteria)

This does not speak to falling into lazy patterns or being irresponsible. This is a recommendation for those who consciously fight with themselves about moving forward into DOing something that may not be in their best interest.

Remember that "Inspired Actions" get better results, are usually easier to take, and keep you in the flow rather than paddling against the current of life.

PLANNING AROUND BARRIERS

After we are intuitively urged to take action or to make a decision, then we can apply specific planning tools that can guide us around barriers to success.

Remember that a plan requires the earlier steps of setting a goal and determining action steps, so this exercise takes you through the entire process.

The best plans are those that anticipate the barriers or blockages and plan around them. For those of us who are tuned into the energetics, we can feel when a plan requires some adjustment in order to lead to success.

For all of you serious energy therapists, sometimes people utilize kinesiology to check on aspects of a plan; others might use a pendulum to check out various components that are being specified within the plan to determine personal congruency with it. Oracles and testing devices, when used appropriately, without energetic bias, can be powerful tools. Those who are not skilled in their use can be very confused by the manipulation of the energetic answers by the user, so these are not to be utilized without experience and skill... and are not necessary in order to benefit from the following exercises.

An easy to use approach to planning around barriers is explained on the following pages... and each step or section builds on the next, so don't be confused by where you think you may led, because all of the steps will be used in the long run.

New Paradigm Goal-Setting...

I. GOAL:

Write out a single goal using description and feelings to make it very specific and clear.

Identify what you choose to accomplish and how you choose to FEEL when you are living the results. - You may want to copy this exercise to use with a variety of separate goals.

II. Inspired Action Steps:

List below action steps that each provide both a logical and inspired step closer to achieving your goal.

1-

2-

3-

4-

5-

6-

7-

8-

9-

10-

III. Indicators of Inner Resistance:

List below fears, blockages, misgivings, negative feelings, blocks that you have about any part of the previous Goals and Action Steps. Be very clear about what part of the goal or action step the perceived blockage is connected to.

1-

2-

3-

4-

5-

6-

7-

8-

9-

10-

IV. Physical Indicators:

List below places in your physical body where you have a reaction to the blockages listed on the previous pages. Think of each and feel your body.

1-

2-

3-

4-

5-

6-

7-

8-

9-

10-

A simple energy exercise that will help ease the reaction is to place one hand on the location where you feel the physical sensation and your other hand across your forehead above your eyebrows. Just hold this position creating a kinesiological circuit and breathe out the charge as you think about each of your resistances.

V. Identifying Opposite Polarities:

List below each perceived blockage from previous pages and list its exact opposite. Put them in the appropriate column based on your perceptions.

Example: "It won't work." – "It will work."

Negative Aspect: **Positive Aspect:**

1-

2-

3-

4-

5-

6-

7-

8-

9-

10-

VI. Cuztic Emotional Release Technique™:

"Cuztic", Mandala by Anne I. Merkel[11]

---

[11] To enlarge this go to:
http://www.arielagroup.com/img/mandala_cuztic.jpg

Using the diagram on the previous page, we will move step-by-step through a congruency-building and emotional release technique involving eye movements to clear energy blocks in the brain and energy field. Do not worry - you will not be overcome by negative emotions or react outwardly in uncomfortable ways. This technique is one that gently accesses various parts of your brain and supports the neutralizing of the "charge" around negative blockages that might otherwise keep you from reaching your goal(s).

The steps you have taken up to this point will be utilized here and you may follow the lines of the picture/ mandala as you move through the exercise. (Also, you may use EFT tapping as you follow the process, but I encourage you to do it without tapping the first time to feel its results.)

Follow these directions for the sequencing of the eye movement steps, and follow the Cuztic Mandala for added results:

1. **Axis #1:** You will move your eyes horizontally from side to side.
2. **Axis #2:** You will move your eyes vertically up and down.
3. **Axis #3:** You will move your eyes diagonally.
4. **Axis #4**: Next you will move your eyes along the other diagonal axis.
5. **Axis #5:** Next move your eyes around the outer edges of your peripheral vision in a circle in one direction.
6. **Axis #6:** Next change directions as you move back around the outer edges of your peripheral vision in a circle.

Here are the steps for this exercise:

Refer to your list of "Indicators of Inner Resistance" that you have previously identified, and the

"Polarities" or opposites that you have stated. It does not matter which end of each axis you consider to be "negative" and which you consider "positive". The focus here is to neutralize both ends of the spectrum so that you become congruent with both of the polarities and everything in between.

In other words, you are neutralizing any emotional charge around either of the polarities... ultimately so you then are left with two options, choices, situations, and you are emotionally clear around both.

When you feel congruent about the full spectrum of aspects and details around an issue, then you hold no charge, and whether or not you agree or disagree with an issue, you can feel at peace so that you can make aligned decisions and take appropriate actions. In setting a goal, if you feel congruent about all aspects of the goal, then it will more easily be brought to fruition.

With your list of polarities you will focus your eyes on one Axis at a time, imagining and feeling one polarity at one end of the axis and the other polarity at the other as you move your eyes from one end to the other of the axis.

Start with Axis #1 and move your eyes back and forth horizontally. At one end of the axis focus on feeling one polarity of an incongruity and then focus on feeling the opposite polarity at the other end of the axis.

Example: Pretend that you have an emotional block about paying a late fee on an overdue bill. One polarity might be the anger, frustration, shame associated with paying late and being charged for it... the other polarity might be the gratitude for having the account, being able to pay late when necessary, and gratitude for being able to pay a little fee for this privilege. Keeping those opposite thoughts with their associated feelings in mind, move your eyes along that first horizontal axis, feeling one polarity at one end, and the other polarity at the other end.

You may start out slowly. After you are accustomed to this exercise your ability to hold the feelings and move your eyes quickly along each axis will improve. When you no longer feel any emotional "charge" or energy around either end of the axis, then you can go to the next axis and do the same thing.

Follow the exercise in order of each axis until you finish by moving your eyes around the outer edges of the big circle, first in one direction and when the charge is released there, then by going in the opposite direction around the circle. Alternately think about one polarity, then the other.

When you have finished the eye movements of Axis #1-6, then go back to the original goal and identify the challenge or blockage that you have just worked with. Is there any more charge around it? If so, then take a different aspect of the same blockage and follow the same procedure of 1-identifying polarities and then 2-going through the eye movement exercises until the charge is released.

Sometimes while focusing on one set of polarities other related thoughts will enter your mind – this is fine – allow them all to align. Keep focusing back on the goal or action step in question and let your mind move from the original polarities to other related issues if it does so naturally. Let the thoughts flow as you keep bringing yourself gently back to the original polarities. By allowing these additional angles of the issue to creep in, you are releasing related charges, and all of it is beneficial to you in the end.

When you feel congruent with an issue, the blockages you identified, and both polarities that you listed, then you will know that the Cuztic Technique™ has worked for you and that you are congruent with all aspects of the goal that you have identified and processed.

You may feel a bit tired or light-headed at the end of performing the Cuztic Technique™, and that is a normal indication that you have released some energetic charge(s) – the purpose of the exercise.

So, in review, the order of the exercise steps are the following:

Step 1 – Holding in your mind the thoughts and feelings around a blockage to attaining a goal, with the opposite polarities of that issue, first move your eyes back and forth along the horizontal axis, focusing on one polarity at one end and the other polarity at the other end of the axis, until you don't feel any more energy around one polarity or the other,

Step 2 – Next, keep focusing on the polarities and the associated feelings as you move your eyes up and down the vertical axis. Keep doing this until you feel no more charge.

Step 3 – Do the same process for the #3 diagonal axis until the charge disappears.

Step 4 – Do the same for the #4 diagonal axis until the charge disappears.

Step 5 – Now go back and forth between the polarities as you move your eyes first around the outer circle in one direction. When the charge is dispelled, then move your eyes around the circle in the opposite direction focusing on one and then the other polarity as you move your eyes around. Do this until the charge is gone.

Using the Cuztic Technique™ will open up your ability to be congruent with various aspects of your goals and their action steps so that they will be easier to achieve.

The Cuztic Technique™ is also very helpful in the decision-making process, where you can compare potential decisions or choices. When you clear all resistance to each, then you can more easily make a clear decision or choice.

I highly recommend this exercise when you feel emotionally pulled in one direction or another and simply want to clearly decide on a goal, decision, or choice.

You can apply the Cuztic Technique™ to a print-out of the mandala above by following the lines of the painting in your eye motions. See the colored axis lines as you focus on the polarity concepts and move your eyes. By using this as your guide you will take in colors that will enervate your charkas or energy centers of your body, which will support balance and alignment. Soon you will be able to do the exercise without using a diagram... moving your eyes the full distance between the edges of your peripheral vision and around the outer edges. Some people prefer eyes open while others prefer eyes shut. This is up to you.

PLANNING TO UTILIZE OPPORTUNITIES

After releasing or neutralizing blockages to successfully achieve your goals, another more traditional, yet beneficial process to utilize that will allow you to evaluate yourself in relation to your goal, is a specialized SWOT analysis.

When you have focused on your vision, set your goals, and been inspired to set and take action steps, then it is time to put this all into your PLAN.

SWOT: Measuring the Plan Strengths, Weaknesses, Opportunities, Threats.

As goals are set and plans are made, it is beneficial to analyze your relationship with the goal(s), action steps, and the over-all plan.

Often we focus more on what could go wrong and where we are incongruent rather than where possible opportunities exist. This balanced exercise looks at your plan from all angles.

Any time you create a plan you have a direct personal relationship with it, so your own dynamics will affect the results of the plan.

The application process here is to:

1. Put a plan into writing;
2. Use the Cuztic Technique™ to take away any lingering charge that you hold around aspects of the plan and its underlying goals;
3. Now apply the SWOT analysis to your relationship with the plan.

You can perform this exercise on notepad paper or larger space such as on a flipchart paper pad. The object is to address the four aspects as they pertain to the plan and goals, also keeping in mind how you are personally related to the plan and goals in each area.

Keep in mind that the more balanced you are in your own life and sense of SELF, the more balanced will be your Plan... for yourself, and ultimately for your practice!

PLAN:

*List here a plan related to one or more aspects
of the NEW life that you are creating.*

Clearing Resistance to the Plan:

Apply the Cuztic™ or Tapping protocols if you feel the least bit of resistance around anything in your plan or in any aspects of this exercise.

Strengths:

What are the strengths of the plan as it is stated? How does your relationship with the plan add strength to its success?

Weaknesses:

What are the weaknesses of the plan as it is stated? How does your relationship with the plan weaken its possibility of success?

Opportunities:

What should you be watching for or can you already anticipate are opportunities that will support the success of your plan?

Threats:

About what should you be wary now and in the future, that could threaten the success of your plan?

Notes:

Add anything that you choose to note here.

Following the previous exercise you should be able to anticipate positive and negative influences on your plan, and adjust it accordingly.

PRIORITIZING AND GOAL-SETTING WITH OTHERS

As the goals are set and plans are designed it is still of importance for you to realize that a full-blown plan doesn't just implement itself overnight. I like the analogy of eating an apple.

When one plans to eat a special apple often it looks almost too big to handle alone. We have to analyze whether the task might require more than one of us to handle it. As the plan unfolds, other players, procedures, techniques, action steps must be considered in order for us to successfully serve our purpose of satisfying our craving for an apple... and then do it successfully so that we can share with the "right" people and not choke ourselves in the process of eating.

Action steps must be incorporated that enable bite sized bits to be nibbled off of the larger plan. One cannot eat a whole apple in one bite!! And, sometimes we cannot expect to eat it alone, so a team focus to planning must take place. Action steps must be reasonable and practical for all concerned,... and they must FEEL RIGHT before we embark on taking them... or "biting them off"!

Completion of the plan is ultimately the focus or planned result of the individuals and the group, however, the most important aspect of planning and goal-setting is creating and participating in the PROCESS. We want it to "work" and we want to be aligned with the process all the way through.

The following grid provides an exercise that can be used individually or with groups or teams. It is helpful in the initial stages of strategic planning, and it is good for visioning and for goal-setting. This technique is based on energy flow and the inter-connectedness of all of the parts as a purpose is grounded and shared, group vision is identified, and then the plan unfolds with all focused on where each individual will best participate and which outside resources are needed.

Follow the numbered steps as you fill in parts of your group plan on the grid. (This can be used for individual plans that require outside support – such as a private energy therapy practice, and it is dynamite in clarifying all that needs to be covered in a group planning & prioritizing process.)

The concept of the "Medicine Wheel" comes from Native American cultures and their focus on the powers of the four directions. Often teams create a planning "banner" or "shield" with colors, symbols, plus more detail within each of the open areas. It can be a fun whole-brain process for all!

"Medicine Wheel" Planning Grid

5-Leadership

Champions/ rules

commitment

4-Management

Barrier removal/

Resources

1-Purpose

Intention/

Big Picture

2-Vision

Focus/ goals

Clarity

3-Community

Population/ Audience

Market/ Issues

To best utilize the "Medicine Wheel"-based planning grid, consider the following things:

#1- Starting in the center, the **PURPOSE** is WHY you are creating the plan, bringing people together, setting the goals that necessitate the plan. By stating an intention here you can GROUND the energies of the plan. Your purpose may be very broad; do not worry, as your more specific focus related to the purpose will be stated clearly in the next visioning step.

#2- Next go to the East, where the sun rises. Here you will create and clarify your shared **VISION**, which is based on the purpose, and specifies the aspect of your purpose that this plan will handle or incorporate. Be as detailed here as is necessary or as feels "right" concerning your plan. Have you verbalized the true essence of what you want your plan to bring about? Have you made it very clear just what aspect of the bigger picture or purpose you will be handling through this plan?

#3- After grounding the purpose and specifying the vision for your team plan, next go to the South and focus on who the plan will serve. Who is the market, client or customer base, recipient of the results of the vision. What population will the plan serve? (This can be clients, neighborhoods, regions, etc.) This step helps you to remember to include all details in the plan that pertain to the **COMMUNITY** with which it is involved. Have you remembered all of the specifics describing who the plan will serve, so that it can be designed appropriately?

#4- Now we go to the West, where details must be handled before the sun goes down. Here is the **MANAGEMENT** segment where details about resources, procedures, other implementation issues must be remembered and listed clearly. Have you remembered all of the details here that will help to support carrying out and maintaining the plan? Do you need to enlist the help of additional support staff or managers to help with this aspect of the plan?

#5- Finally we go to the North, where **LEADERSHIP** supports the plan. Who are the individuals or groups who will champion the plan? Who will support and implement the rules and help to build commitment from the rest of the team? Have you included all of the plan details related to this area? Are YOU the leader (in your practice, for example), or do you report to someone else who plays that role. Sometimes this role must be assigned to a person or team with specialized leadership skills to enable you to perform as the energy therapist or other practitioner of your own skills. Make sure to clarify who will best handle the leadership role.

Using this model for planning helps you to think in a Whole Brain way, as you consider various aspects of the plan and how it will actually function as a guiding organism involving a team. This can be used as the primary strategic planning tool or in conjunction with other planning templates for business, practice, or project planning.

TAKING INSPIRED ACTIONS

We have already talked about the process of **BE ->
HAVE -> DO** in creating a NEW LIFE. We have
discussed how when we are BEing ourselves, feeling
that we HAVE that to which we aspire, then we will be
inspired to DO the tasks that reap the highest and
best rewards.

In order to place this process into action and "amp up"
the speed and new habit-building properties that will
aid in your successful DELIBERATE CREATION of your
NEW LIFE and/or PRACTICE, I would like to share
some tips that can accelerate and support you to Flow
Forward.

1. Create and Maintain an Abundant Mindset

You will create more of whatever you focus on
consistently. Make it your deliberate intention to take
inspired action to focus on the positive aspects and

feelings of what you are DELIBERATELY CREATING, several times a day.

If you desire to experience Wealth and Abundance you must THINK like the wealthy, dream abundant thoughts, and align yourself with people who share these attitudes!! Instead of focusing on the gap between where you are NOW and where you WANT TO BE, consciously focus your thoughts and feelings – numerous times each day – on how it is to HAVE that NEW LIFE NOW!!

If you want to participate in a wonderful relationship, then you can start by being in a wonderful relationship with YOURSELF – NOW! Learn how a wonderful relationship feels, and languish in these feelings, daily!

If you desire happiness, then you must look for the good in your present life and focus on what makes you happy NOW!! Be in the moment and state your gratitude for the things that make you happy.

When you have conditioned your mind to focus on happiness, prosperity, abundance, all of the aspects of your NEW REALITY, then MORE of that will be automatically attracted to you.

2. Be Conscious of your Energy at ALL TIMES

Our minds naturally wander, and when we dwell on thoughts of lack, loss, negativity, then we are contradicting all of the positive thoughts we are learning to focus on. We are blocking our own flow when we unconsciously drop back into old habits of low vibrational thoughts.

Consciously managing your energies - physical, mental, emotional, spiritual, money, time - is the foundation upon which your NEW LIFE is laid. If you recklessly expend any of these energies, then you are sabotaging yourself.

In the case of money, if you do not pay bills on time, have no idea of what money comes in and what goes out, then on a subconscious level you could actually be repelling wealth. You may be pushing it out of your experience because deep inside, you realize you would not know how to handle more money even if you had it.

In the case of emotions, if you are wasting your emotional energy on nostalgic thoughts of the past or longings for the future, then you are wasting the present. NOW is when you can be manifesting into your life the dreams to create that future and let go of the past.

In the case of mental energy, learn to control your thoughts. Where your attention goes, energy flows. Make sure you focus on the positive things that you WANT to manifest into your life.

You will be amazed at how you 'magically' tap into MORE prosperity and abundance when you become a master at managing your energies! This is definitely an inspired action step to put into your daily life.

3. Constantly SEE and FEEL your NEW LIFE

Visualizing and feeling whatever you desire in your life, as though it were already there, will accelerate attracting that into your experience at lightening speed. SEE and FEEL yourself already being in the relationship of your dreams, using the things you bought with your mountains of money wealth, living in the house you built with your abundant income, driving the car you purchased with your own cash. KNOW what it feels like to BE in the state of already HAVEing that which you most desire.

Enjoy visualizing and FEELING the joy and peace of mind that comes from living in your NEW REALITY. For faster results, add delicious feelings of love, satisfaction, and gratitude at the same time that you project yourself living your NEW LIFE.

4. Be constantly GRATEFUL for what you HAVE NOW

Gratitude is one of the most powerful, yet underestimated manifestation tools that you can apply. The more grateful you feel, the more you will receive to be grateful for.

In applying the inspired actions associated with gratitude you can begin to feel the difference in your attitude, which can shift your energetics and help you to attract more positive results into your life.

Even though this can be a challenging concept if you are currently experiencing financial or personal hardship, pay attention to the concept of the "Attitude of Gratitude", because this is what can change your life around quickly.

At the end of each day, take inspired action to write down at least 5-10 things you are grateful for. This can include anything you think of: thoughts, feelings, sunshine on the water, birds singing in the trees, accomplishments and successes from that day, the fact that the day is over and it's time for bed.   Do this consistently for the next 60 days and you will be amazed at the abundance that begins to flow into your life.

5. Take Inspired Actions that make you FEEL the Abundance

You can feel the abundance in all areas of your life if you make a concerted and conscious effort to do so.

You can feel abundance in the caliber of relationships in your life, the amount of money you circulate through your system, the number of "things" that surround you in your lifestyle, the blessings that you receive each day in big and small ways. When you consciously practice FEELING the abundance in one or more areas of your life, then it starts to become a habit that attracts all of the "right" components to create an abundant NEW REALITY.

Take inspired actions that you KNOW will help you to FEEL the abundance all around you! Have a massage, surround yourself with fresh flowers, go to a day spa, hire a luxury car, go to a fancy restaurant, have someone come in to clean your house, take your best friends out to lunch. Whatever can help you FEEL the abundance will work here. The more you practice taking the inspired actions to FEEL the abundance, the faster you attract MORE!!

6. Create a space for the Abundance to FLOW IN!!

The Universe abhors a vacuum. Take inspired actions to create open spaces for more abundance, and it will soon flood in to fill the openings. Clear out unnecessary clutter in your life – the books that you don't read, the paperwork in your drawers, the old clothes that no longer fit, the boxes of junk in the garage, the habits that no longer serve your lifestyle.

When you clean out the old, you make room for the new. Start creating that space for abundance today.

7. Have FUN!! – Laugh!! – Play!!

One of the most important things that you can do on a daily basis to move easily and effortlessly into the flow of abundance is to place FUN into your life. Your experience of life is the result of your attitude!!

Having fun moves your energy into a place of attraction, so practice the following inspired action:

Before undertaking any task, be it business or personal, take a moment to FEEL. Do you feel light inside? Does the thought of the task seem easy? Are you looking forward to doing whatever it is? Will it be FUN to perform the task?? - If not, then how can you adjust the task so that it FEELS better to you?? With the intention of getting to the end result, how can you perform the task differently and have more FUN while getting the same results?? Some tasks may take more soul-searching than others, but in the long run, by taking a pause to align yourself with each task, you are then able to create a win-win-win situation for all concerned.

When you find yourself in a FUN situation, use that time wisely to attract to you the prosperity that you desire. When you are having a good time watching a funny movie, playing with your children, spending time with your friends, dancing, genuinely enjoying yourself; while you are in that wonderfully light, funny space, FEEL yourself "abundant" in all ways, and ENJOY it. You may wish to "tap it in" also.

8. Celebrate your Abundance!

Celebration is an integral part of the manifestation process. When we experience our own abundance we can flow into the "attitude of gratitude" and then CELEBRATE!! This just sets the stage to attract more!!

Some people have special celebrations and some just shout "Thank you!!" to the Universe every time more prosperity flows their way. When you have the "right" attitude, every small blessing is something to celebrate. The subconscious mind doesn't know the difference between receiving one cent and $1,000,000, as long as you are happy and grateful!!

9. Share your good fortune

Tithing is an age-old secret that millionaires practice. Most did not wait until they were rich to begin tithing, they took inspired actions and did it before, during, and after they accumulated their wealth.

Universal Law states that the more you give of something, the more you receive. If you want more smiles, give more smiles, if you want more love, give more love, if you want more money, give more money.

Traditionally, tithing means to contribute 10% of all you earn to the person, place, or institution that feeds you spiritually. Give to organizations or individuals with whom you are aligned!

Whenever you give money or service to others, bless it and trust it will return back to you – multiplied!! When you do this you will be amazed at the abundance that pours into your life.

10. Prosperity is part of every aspect of your NEW REALITY

Prosperity and abundance lose their glow if you don't have your health, passion, loved ones in your life, and a special something to do each day that makes your heart sing. A life of prosperity and abundance really IS possible.

How would you feel if you could spend each day with friends that inspire and uplift you, only work because you love what you do, be able to spend your time doing what you choose – when you choose, and continue to experience greater and greater levels of abundance, wealth, prosperity, and JOY year after year??

When you continually and persistently focus your attitude and passion to create your NEW LIFE, daily declare your gratitude, manage your energies wisely, visualize and feel abundant, clean up your clutter, laugh, celebrate, and share your wealth, you will unleash a flow of prosperity that will change your life. That is when you will INTENTIONALLY CREATE your NEW REALITY.

So, are these inspired actions worth your effort??

You can BET they are!! Try them and see for yourself!!

SELF ADVANCEMENT JOURNALING

We have covered a number of exercises and daily practices that you can apply to intentionally create your NEW LIFE. There are two more daily inspired actions I would like to suggest that you consider placing into your list of new habits.

At the start and end of each day are two potent periods of time to set quality energetics in motion.

Each morning I first write in my dream journal if I remember what messages my subconscious has sent me for the day. Next I consciously focus on an exercise that some call "scripting", where I write down a SCRIPT for the upcoming day's activities, feelings, successes, encounters with others, etc.

I list positive outcomes that I anticipate, wonderful feelings that I expect, fun encounters, exciting adventures, wonderfully successful results to projects, among many other aspects of each day.

I write my intentions as though they have already happened, complete with what happened, how I felt, how grateful I was, the excitement of being in that state of abundance in all areas of my life. I script ONLY positive outcomes and feelings, and in doing this, I anticipate and "hold the form" for all of what I write to happen later in the day.

I have found that it is most beneficial to list my FEELINGS around an item rather than listing all of the details. By setting the stage by anticipating FEELINGS without all of the data, then the Universe can fill in the blanks and take care of the minute details.

Even if the exact expected outcomes do not happen, I have found "scripting" helps to create my acceptance of outcomes, and usually results in equal or better outcomes than I had expected. Just leave it up to the Universe to take care of putting everything into motion better than we could ever manipulate the details... and be grateful that you don't have to handle it ALL.

Each evening I write in my journal using a "gratitude format". Where I could simply record the high points of each day, instead I write "I am grateful for ------, " as I list the various activities, encounters, break-throughs, thoughts of the day. I notice that this practice is an easy way to raise my vibrational frequency and shift my mood – even if I am very tired at the end of the day.

Each evening I also fill out the details listed on a manifestation sheet that I have attached in the next section. This sheet has a gratitude section as well as several other key areas that help one in the abundance-attracting process. This is a good exercise sheet, especially for those who do not keep a personal journal.

By ending the day with positive, grateful, anticipatory thoughts, I have found that my sleep is more peaceful, my dreams more positive, and my waking mood more capable of attracting and creating the best NEW REALITY imaginable!! And, over the years of utilizing sheets such as those listed for you on the following pages I have seen my dreams become true manifestations so that I am now living the life that I KNOW I created through conscious visioning, scripting, and journaling processes.

I urge you to consider implementing these daily a.m. and p.m. practices into your life... and you may even consider creating a separate page for your practice. Each exercise takes very little time, and the mental and emotional results are well worth taking 5-15 minutes each morning and evening to focus on positive thoughts and feelings that will shift your life.

My coaching clients follow my lead in implementing these daily "rituals" and their new habits have proven over and over to produce positive results for all who take a little bit of time for themselves and their NEW LIVES.

Remember that a new "habit" or "way of thinking" will take hold if you practice something for at least twenty-one days. For this reason I have provided one month's worth of journaling sheets for you to use as you are creating your new life.

Self Advancement Journal

The form on the next pages can be copied, adapted, added to. Please feel free to customize it for yourself. It must FEEL comfortable in order for you to want to use it each evening before you go to bed.

Many of the concepts covered earlier in this book are reinforced in this form. After you have used it for at least 21 days it will become an easy habit. Until then, think of filling it in each night as an Inspired Action... and remember – this is for YOU!!

"I am flowing with gratitude, trust, inspiration, - knowing my intentions are being handled by Spirit... and I am inspired and guided to easily move forward in my life!"

Daily Manifestation Sheet for____/____/____,

I am grateful for:

   because:

I choose these goals:

   in order to:

I release these blocks that created resistance to attaining my goals:

I am worthy of attaining my goals because:

I am feeling these emotions as I visualize and FEEL myself LIVING the goal results:

I am inspired & guided to easily take these steps:

Daily Manifestation Sheet for____/____/____,

I am grateful for:

    because:

I choose these goals:

    in order to:

I release these blocks that created resistance to attaining my goals:

I am worthy of attaining my goals because:

I am feeling these emotions as I visualize and FEEL myself LIVING the goal results:

I am inspired & guided to easily take these steps:

Daily Manifestation Sheet for ___/ ___/ ___,

I am grateful for:

because:

I choose these goals:

in order to:

I release these blocks that created resistance to attaining my goals:

I am worthy of attaining my goals because:

I am feeling these emotions as I visualize and FEEL myself LIVING the goal results:

I am inspired & guided to easily take these steps:

Daily Manifestation Sheet for____/____/____,

I am grateful for:

     because:

I choose these goals:

     in order to:

I release these blocks that created resistance to attaining my goals:

I am worthy of attaining my goals because:

I am feeling these emotions as I visualize and FEEL myself LIVING the goal results:

I am inspired & guided to easily take these steps:

Daily Manifestation Sheet for___/___/___,

I am grateful for:

    because:

I choose these goals:

    in order to:

I release these blocks that created resistance to attaining my goals:

I am worthy of attaining my goals because:

I am feeling these emotions as I visualize and FEEL myself LIVING the goal results:

I am inspired & guided to easily take these steps:

Daily Manifestation Sheet for____/____/____,

I am grateful for:

 because:

I choose these goals:

 in order to:

I release these blocks that created resistance to attaining my goals:

I am worthy of attaining my goals because:

I am feeling these emotions as I visualize and FEEL myself LIVING the goal results:

I am inspired & guided to easily take these steps:

Daily Manifestation Sheet for____/____/____,

I am grateful for:

      because:

I choose these goals:

      in order to:

I release these blocks that created resistance to attaining my goals:

I am worthy of attaining my goals because:

I am feeling these emotions as I visualize and FEEL myself LIVING the goal results:

I am inspired & guided to easily take these steps:

Daily Manifestation Sheet for___/___/___,

I am grateful for:

    because:

I choose these goals:

    in order to:

I release these blocks that created resistance to attaining my goals:

I am worthy of attaining my goals because:

I am feeling these emotions as I visualize and FEEL myself LIVING the goal results:

I am inspired & guided to easily take these steps:

Daily Manifestation Sheet for___/___/___,

I am grateful for:

    because:

I choose these goals:

    in order to:

I release these blocks that created resistance to attaining my goals:

I am worthy of attaining my goals because:

I am feeling these emotions as I visualize and FEEL myself LIVING the goal results:

I am inspired & guided to easily take these steps:

Daily Manifestation Sheet for___/___/___,

I am grateful for:

because:

I choose these goals:

in order to:

I release these blocks that created resistance to attaining my goals:

I am worthy of attaining my goals because:

I am feeling these emotions as I visualize and FEEL myself LIVING the goal results:

I am inspired & guided to easily take these steps:

Daily Manifestation Sheet for___/___/___,

I am grateful for:

   because:

I choose these goals:

   in order to:

I release these blocks that created resistance to attaining my goals:

I am worthy of attaining my goals because:

I am feeling these emotions as I visualize and FEEL myself LIVING the goal results:

I am inspired & guided to easily take these steps:

Daily Manifestation Sheet for___/___/___,

I am grateful for:

    because:

I choose these goals:

    in order to:

I release these blocks that created resistance to attaining my goals:

I am worthy of attaining my goals because:

I am feeling these emotions as I visualize and FEEL myself LIVING the goal results:

I am inspired & guided to easily take these steps:

Daily Manifestation Sheet for____/____/____,

I am grateful for:

because:

I choose these goals:

in order to:

I release these blocks that created resistance to attaining my goals:

I am worthy of attaining my goals because:

I am feeling these emotions as I visualize and FEEL myself LIVING the goal results:

I am inspired & guided to easily take these steps:

Daily Manifestation Sheet for____/____/____,

I am grateful for:

       because:

I choose these goals:

       in order to:

I release these blocks that created resistance to attaining my goals:

I am worthy of attaining my goals because:

I am feeling these emotions as I visualize and FEEL myself LIVING the goal results:

I am inspired & guided to easily take these steps:

Daily Manifestation Sheet for___/___/___,

I am grateful for:

    because:

I choose these goals:

    in order to:

I release these blocks that created resistance to attaining my goals:

I am worthy of attaining my goals because:

I am feeling these emotions as I visualize and FEEL myself LIVING the goal results:

I am inspired & guided to easily take these steps:

Daily Manifestation Sheet for___/___/___,

I am grateful for:

    because:

I choose these goals:

    in order to:

I release these blocks that created resistance to attaining my goals:

I am worthy of attaining my goals because:

I am feeling these emotions as I visualize and FEEL myself LIVING the goal results:

I am inspired & guided to easily take these steps:

Daily Manifestation Sheet for___/___/___,

I am grateful for:

    because:

I choose these goals:

    in order to:

I release these blocks that created resistance to attaining my goals:

I am worthy of attaining my goals because:

I am feeling these emotions as I visualize and FEEL myself LIVING the goal results:

I am inspired & guided to easily take these steps:

Daily Manifestation Sheet for____/____/____,

I am grateful for:

    because:

I choose these goals:

    in order to:

I release these blocks that created resistance to attaining my goals:

I am worthy of attaining my goals because:

I am feeling these emotions as I visualize and FEEL myself LIVING the goal results:

I am inspired & guided to easily take these steps:

Daily Manifestation Sheet for___/___/___,

I am grateful for:

because:

I choose these goals:

in order to:

I release these blocks that created resistance to attaining my goals:

I am worthy of attaining my goals because:

I am feeling these emotions as I visualize and FEEL myself LIVING the goal results:

I am inspired & guided to easily take these steps:

Daily Manifestation Sheet for____/____/____,

I am grateful for:

    because:

I choose these goals:

    in order to:

I release these blocks that created resistance to attaining my goals:

I am worthy of attaining my goals because:

I am feeling these emotions as I visualize and FEEL myself LIVING the goal results:

I am inspired & guided to easily take these steps:

Daily Manifestation Sheet for____/____/____,

I am grateful for:

    because:

I choose these goals:

    in order to:

I release these blocks that created resistance to attaining my goals:

I am worthy of attaining my goals because:

I am feeling these emotions as I visualize and FEEL myself LIVING the goal results:

I am inspired & guided to easily take these steps:

Daily Manifestation Sheet for___/___/___,

I am grateful for:

    because:

I choose these goals:

    in order to:

I release these blocks that created resistance to attaining my goals:

I am worthy of attaining my goals because:

I am feeling these emotions as I visualize and FEEL myself LIVING the goal results:

I am inspired & guided to easily take these steps:

Daily Manifestation Sheet for___/___/___,

I am grateful for:

  because:

I choose these goals:

  in order to:

I release these blocks that created resistance to attaining my goals:

I am worthy of attaining my goals because:

I am feeling these emotions as I visualize and FEEL myself LIVING the goal results:

I am inspired & guided to easily take these steps:

Daily Manifestation Sheet for___/___/___,

I am grateful for:

      because:

I choose these goals:

      in order to:

I release these blocks that created resistance to attaining my goals:

I am worthy of attaining my goals because:

I am feeling these emotions as I visualize and FEEL myself LIVING the goal results:

I am inspired & guided to easily take these steps:

Daily Manifestation Sheet for____/____/____,

I am grateful for:

      because:

I choose these goals:

      in order to:

I release these blocks that created resistance to attaining my goals:

I am worthy of attaining my goals because:

I am feeling these emotions as I visualize and FEEL myself LIVING the goal results:

I am inspired & guided to easily take these steps:

Daily Manifestation Sheet for ___/___/___,

I am grateful for:

    because:

I choose these goals:

    in order to:

I release these blocks that created resistance to attaining my goals:

I am worthy of attaining my goals because:

I am feeling these emotions as I visualize and FEEL myself LIVING the goal results:

I am inspired & guided to easily take these steps:

Daily Manifestation Sheet for ____/____/____,

I am grateful for:

    because:

I choose these goals:

    in order to:

I release these blocks that created resistance to attaining my goals:

I am worthy of attaining my goals because:

I am feeling these emotions as I visualize and FEEL myself LIVING the goal results:

I am inspired & guided to easily take these steps:

Daily Manifestation Sheet for___/___/___,

I am grateful for:

      because:

I choose these goals:

      in order to:

I release these blocks that created resistance to attaining my goals:

I am worthy of attaining my goals because:

I am feeling these emotions as I visualize and FEEL myself LIVING the goal results:

I am inspired & guided to easily take these steps:

Daily Manifestation Sheet for___/___/___,

I am grateful for:

    because:

I choose these goals:

    in order to:

I release these blocks that created resistance to
attaining my goals:

I am worthy of attaining my goals because:

I am feeling these emotions as I visualize and FEEL
myself LIVING the goal results:

I am inspired & guided to easily take these steps:

Daily Manifestation Sheet for____/____/____,

I am grateful for:

    because:

I choose these goals:

    in order to:

I release these blocks that created resistance to attaining my goals:

I am worthy of attaining my goals because:

I am feeling these emotions as I visualize and FEEL myself LIVING the goal results:

I am inspired & guided to easily take these steps:

Daily Manifestation Sheet for____/____/____,

I am grateful for:

    because:

I choose these goals:

    in order to:

I release these blocks that created resistance to attaining my goals:

I am worthy of attaining my goals because:

I am feeling these emotions as I visualize and FEEL myself LIVING the goal results:

I am inspired & guided to easily take these steps:

FINAL WORDS

Thank you, reader, for walking this way with me. I hope you have been inspired by something that I have shared with you here.

The exercises and attitudes expressed in this book have been tested by me, my coaching clients, and other EFT & Energy Therapy Practitioners. We have seen the transformation in our lives and invite you to begin to see miracles occur in your own.

I wish you well on your journey of opening fully to the abundance all around you. Today is a perfect time to FLOW FORWARD and create that NEW REALITY that meets all of your expectations.

Only YOU can prove that the exercises that I have listed in this book will work for you. Take inspired action, and see what positive transformation happens in your life!

STEPS FOR THE FUTURE

If you would like to walk further with me, then check out the following <u>special programs</u> for Health & Wellness Practitioners, Physicians, Coaches, as well as EFT Tapping Enthusiasts and Self-Growth Practitioners:

EFT & Energy Therapy Practitioners' Mastermind Series:[12]

This program offers two live calls per month where you connect with like-minded others, share cases, strategies, tips, and learn to "go deeper" with your clients or patients. This is a learning, sharing, intention-setting opportunity for you with other health & wellness practitioners who use Energy Therapy modalities in their practices. We use EFT plus many other energy therapy modalities in the live calls.

---

[12] To learn more go to: http://arielagroup.com/mastermind

Energy Therapy Practitioner Certification Program:[13]

This six-month personalized program is meant for all Health & Wellness as well as Self-Growth Practitioners and EFT Practitioners who would like to add or perfect the use of Energy Therapy modalities in an on-going or new practice. Included in this one-on-one program:

- Personal coaching with Energy modalities to help you be the best practitioner and person that you can be,
- Instruction in various Energy Therapy, Energy Medicine, Kinesiology, and Naturopathic techniques to support you to further your support of your clients,
- Support in setting up or stream-lining your practice in the areas of marketing, social media, session design, office lay-out, etc.

---

[13] Check out: http://arielagroup.com/energy-therapy-certification

- Inclusion in the twice-monthly Practitioner Mastermind live calls,
- Extensive recordings, books, a full training manual, open e-mail access to Anne Merkel, and so much more!

Transformative Coach Training for Energy Therapy Practitioners:[14]

This two-month program focuses on providing a strong foundation in Coaching fundamentals for Energy Therapy Practitioners who would like to add more structure to their practices. This program includes both individual and group sessions, and graduates will find that their Energy Therapy practices and sessions flow more fluidly with greater client results.

---

[14] Learn more at: http://www.myeftcoach.com/practitioner-coach-training

ADDITIONAL RESOURCES

Look on **Amazon** for more specialized texts for EFT & Energy Therapy Practitioners by this author... including:

- *EFT- Best Practices for Energy Management*
  and
- *Transformative Coaching Guide for EFT & Energy Therapy Practitioners*

*And, if you enjoyed this book, you may also wish to check out our **Wholistic Products & Services**[15] collection at* <u>www.ArielaGroup.com</u> .

Printed in Great Britain
by Amazon